PLANET DEXTER'S

pattern block city!

The Best Pattern Block Activities Ever!

Includes 32 Pattern Blocks!

Fun for Kids!

No Sweat for Parents!

The Editors of Planet Dexter
A Planet Dexter, Jr. Book

PLANET DEXTER

SCHOLASTIC INC.

New York   Toronto   London   Auckland   Sydney

ISBN 0-590-97223-5

12 11 10 9 8 7 6 5 4   8 9/9 0 1 2/0

Printed in the U.S.A.   08

First Scholastic printing, February 1997

And now a Message from Our Corporate Lawyer:

▼

"Neither the Publisher nor the Author shall be liable for any damage that may be caused or sustained as a result of conducting any of the activities in this book without specifically following instructions, conducting the activities without proper supervision, or ignoring the cautions contained in the book."

acknowledgments

▶

Chris St. Cyr, Sharon Broll, John Bell, Bonnie Gale, Christa Benjamin, Erin Sweeney, Heather Mimnaugh, and the team at Proof Positive/Farrowlyne Associates, Inc.

A Planet Dexter Sort of Introduction

Hi.

Welcome to Planet Dexter (where kids jump twice as high and grown-ups don't sweat) . . . and Pattern Blocks.

Pattern Blocks come in six beautiful colors and geometric shapes, and are used in class-rooms throughout the world. Pattern Blocks gently introduce kids to the fundamental geometric concepts of angles and spatial relationships, while encouraging exploration and artistic and mathematical creation. Because the blocks are colorful, tactile, and fun to play with, children don't realize the direct mathematical lessons that the blocks are imparting—lessons dealing with symmetry, area, perimeter, congruence, fractions, similarity, patterns, graphing, and counting (on Planet Dexter, this is what's known as "stealth learning").

Anyway, that's the theory behind the use of Pattern Blocks in schools. It's also *all* the theory any average grown-up (parent, child-care provider, relative, baby-sitter, older sibling, etc.) in any kid's life needs to know. The real value of *Pattern Block City!* is the opportunity it provides to play around with a kid, to have valuable fun—while at school, home, on the beach, or stuck in the car.

With the simple play suggested by this book—which is authored by a team of really nice people who are also educators and parents—children explore, match, estimate, build, measure, sort, and learn about patterns and symmetry. Just remember that *Pattern Block City!* is supposed to be enjoyable. So if you don't like *Pattern Block City!*, please let us know. Seriously! Or better yet, let us know what you do like about this book. We'd like to be able to incorporate your sug-gestions in future books. Really!

You can write to us at the following address:

The Editors of Planet Dexter
Addison-Wesley Publishing Company
One Jacob Way
Reading, MA 01867

Comments may be faxed to us at
(617) 944-8243

You can contact us via the Internet at
pdexter@aw.com

or America Online at
PDexter

We do hope that you'll enjoy *Pattern Block City!* and that we'll hear from you soon. And remember, on Planet Dexter everybody's brain holds twice as much.

—The Editors of Planet Dexter

Kids' Tour of Pattern Block City

today's tour guides:

Harvey · Helen · Hubert · Hannah · Herschel

Hailey · Horace · Heather · Hector · Henrietta · Hayward

Homer · Hillary · Henry · Heidi · Hermosa

what you'll see: our favorite spots

what to bring:

next tour leaves: right now!

Cover the spaces. Use
1 block for each space.

HEATHER

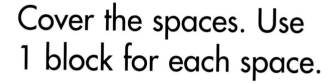

Moo shu is not something
a cow wears. It is something
you can order at my favorite
restaurant in Chinatown.

Cover the spaces. Use
1 block for each space.

HORACE

If you like fruits and
vegetables, you will love the
Farmers' Market.

Cover the spaces. Use
1 block for each space.

HERMOSA

My favorite part of the
city is Triangle Square.
That's where all the cool
shops are.

10

Cover the spaces. Use
1 block for each space.

HERMOSA

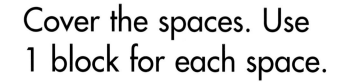

Some of the shops have
funny names. This one is
called Sew What.

Cover the spaces. Use
1 block for each space.

HELEN

Myrtle's World of Turtles
only sells one thing. Can
you guess what it is?

How good is *your* memory?
Look at this design. Then
cover up the design. Can
you build what you just
saw?

HECTOR

This is a neat store. Too
bad I can't remember how
to get to it.

16

Cover the spaces. Use
1 block for each space.

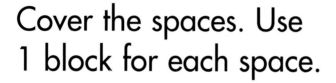

HAILEY

It's easy to tell where
famous people live. Just
look for the paparazzi.
(That's not a place for Italian
food. It's another word for
"photographers.")

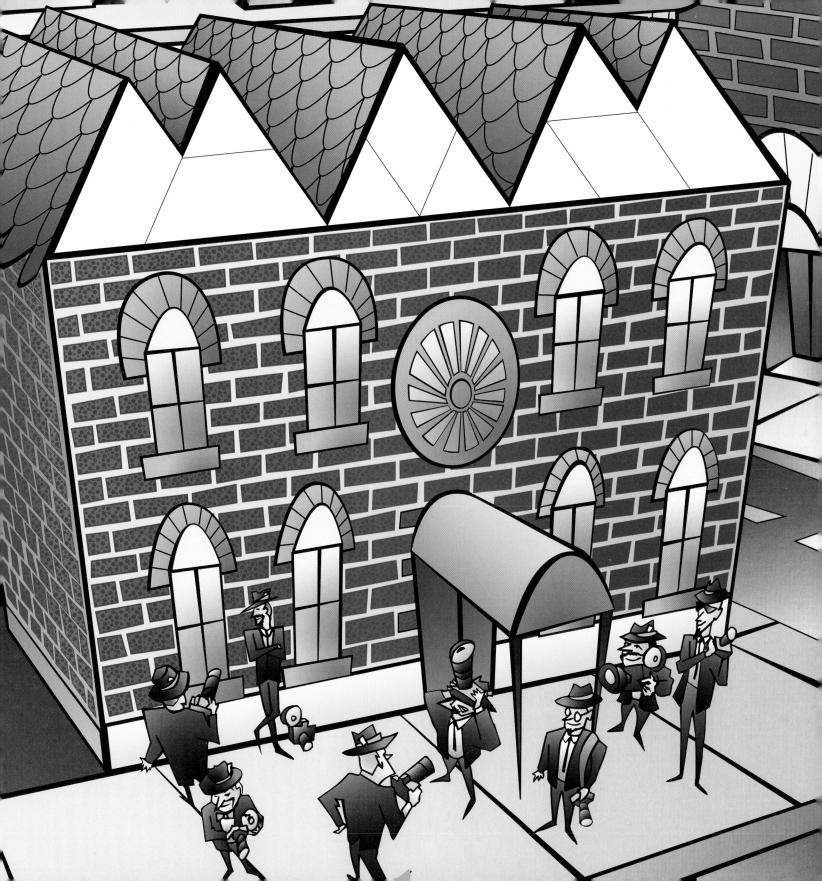

Cover up the bonsai tree.
Use any blocks you want.

HAYWARD

The sidewalk is like a giant store. You can buy ice cream, hot dogs, T-shirts, even tiny bonsai trees.

Two workers were making a pattern around this yellow tile. Then they took a break. Use blocks to show how the workers will finish the pattern.

HELEN

The sidewalks on this street have colorful designs. (At least they will by the time you get here.)

Cover up the kite with blocks.
Use only 1 color.

Now use 2 colors to cover
up the kite.

Can you cover up the
kite with 3 colors?

HENRY

All around the park are
tall buildings. Some of the
buildings are hotels. If you
stay in one, this is what
you might see when you
look out the window.

Cover up the basketball. Use any blocks you want.

HEIDI

The arena has concerts, rodeos, circuses, ice shows, and more. I think basketball games there are the most fun.

Cover the sailboat with blocks. Use any colors you want.

HERSCHEL

There is a small park near the marina. I like to sit there and watch the boats.

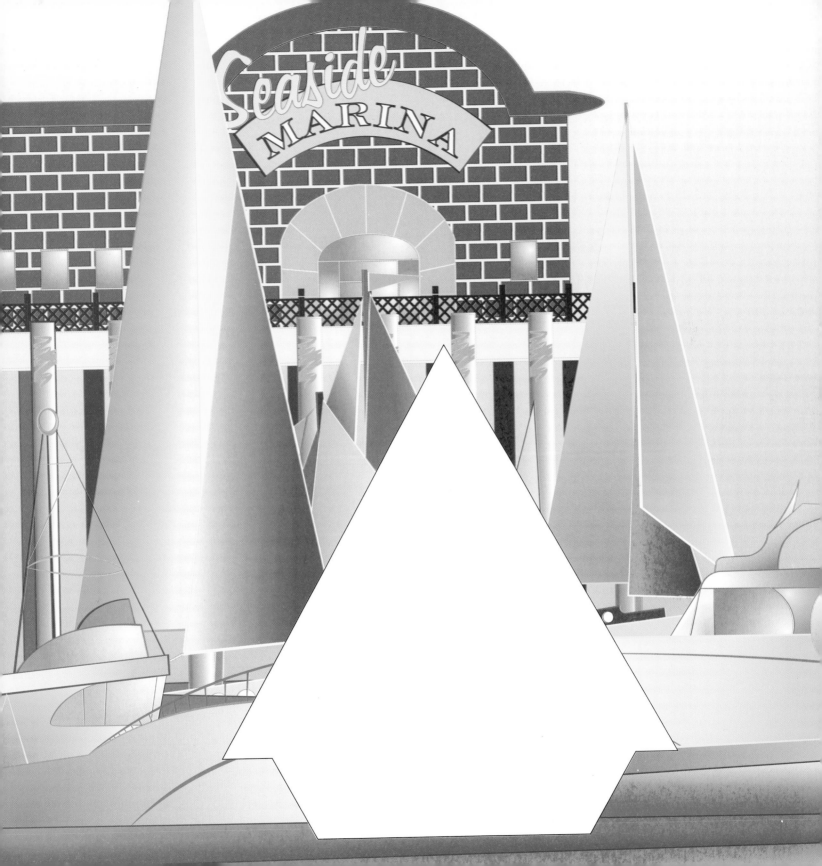

Use exactly 7 blocks to cover up the star. Then try it with 6 blocks.

HANNAH

You can see more stars here during the day than at night. (But you have to know where to look.)

Cover up the light with 5 blocks.

Can you think of 2 other ways to cover up the light with 5 blocks?

HANNAH

Don't be surprised if you also see another kind of star. Hey, isn't that guy on TV?

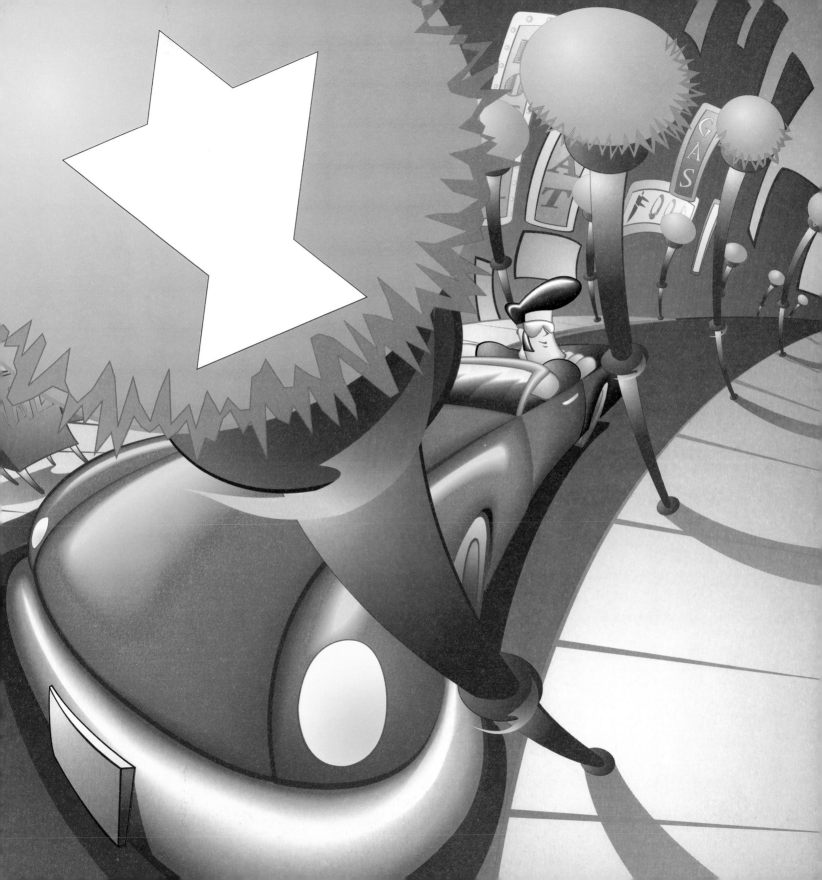

Cover up the bridge with blocks. Use any colors you want.

HOMER

The zoo is near Polygon Park. Here is how to get there: First, cross over the old stone bridge . . .

What 2 shapes go next?
Put down 2 blocks to
continue the pattern.

HOMER

. . . then follow the
shapes on the sidewalk to
the zoo entrance.

36

Cover up the penguin.

Can you think of a different way to cover up the penguin?

HILLARY

The penguins are always fun to watch. I like it when they slide on their bellies.

38

Cover up the fox with blocks. Use any colors you want.

Can you find the smallest number of blocks it takes to cover up the fox?

HUBERT

You might not see any foxes. My favorite fox spends a lot of time sleeping in a hollow log.

Cover up the gargoyle. Use as many blocks as you can.

HARVEY

A gargle is a sound you can make with mouthwash. A gargoyle is a scary stone creature. Old buildings are the best place to spot them.

Cover up the dinosaur's jaws and teeth. Use any blocks you want.

HECTOR

The zoo is not the only place to learn about animals. At the Museum of Natural History, I found out that the word dinosaur means "terrible lizard."

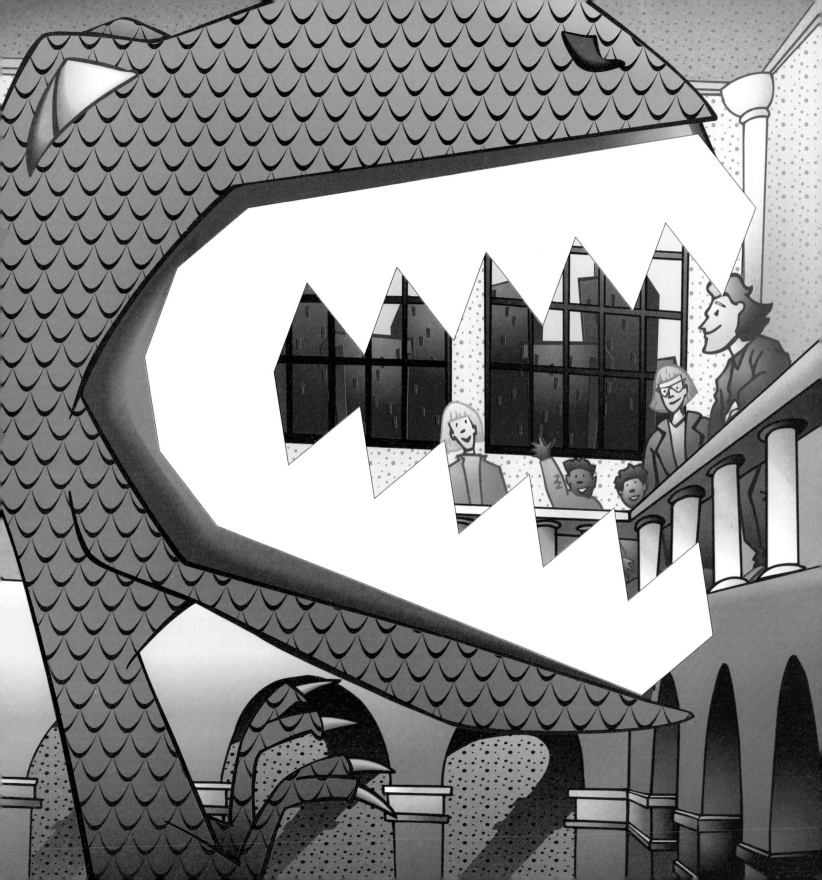

Cover up the opera singer's hat. Use any blocks you want.

HENRIETTA

The costumes are the best thing about the opera. Check out that hat!

46

Hey, Good News! More Planet Dexter, Jr. Books!

Wow! We suggest the following "All-Time, Best-Ever Planet Dexter, Jr. Favorites," for kids ages 4 to 7. (They should be available at whatever bookstore you like to use. If not, the bookstore can always order them for you. Enjoy!)

The All-Time, Best-Ever Planet Dexter, Jr. Favorites

PLANET DEXTER'S RODS, RODS, RODS
Includes 37 assorted Cuisenaire® Rods

HOW HIGH IS PEPPERONI?
The Planet Dexter Book — and Tape! — of Highs, Longs, and Arounds!
Includes a Dexterized measuring tape and Dexterized marker

RODDY!
The Best Rod Activities Ever! Fun for Kids! No Sweat for Parents!
Includes 55 Cuisenaire® Rods